FLUSH

RUSH

FLUSH
RUSH

Brian Keliher
Illustrations by C. Laurin

TEN SPEED PRESS
Berkeley, California

1🠒

TEN SPEED PRESS
P.O. Box 7123
Berkeley, CA 94707

Cover design by Fifth Street Design, Berkeley, California
Text design by Studioads, Albany, California

Library of Congress Cataloging-in-Publication Data
Keliher, Brian.
        Flush Rush / Brian Keliher ; cartoons by C. Laurin.
              p. cm.
         ISBN 0-89815-610-6
         1. Limbaugh, Rush H. I. Laurin, C. II. Title.
       PN1991.4.L48K45 1994
       791.44' 028'092–dc20   94-12831
FIRST PRINTING 1994   CIP
Printed in the United States of America
1 2 3 4 5 — 98 97 96 95 94

This collection of the words and wisdom of the Great White One is dedicated to the "feminazis," "environmentalist wackos," "animal rights idiots," and all others on the receiving end of Rush Limbaugh's attacks.

66 At some point in America's future, the house in which I was born will be a shrine. And this building will become a national monument and my birthday will become a national holiday. **99**

–Rush Limbaugh

acknowledgments

It would not have been possible to flush Rush without the assistance of some very special people. We thank: Christine Carswell, Mariah Bear, and Jo Ann Deck of Ten Speed Press, Richard Deck, David Keliher, C. Laurin, Alan Keliher, Paget Norton, Norm Cooper, and Jeff Cohen of FAIR. And a special thanks to all those readers of the *Flush Rush Quarterly* out there who keep us abreast of Rush Limbaugh's antics in their part of The Fruited Plain.

Who Is Rush Limbaugh?

Is he, as he likes to call himself, "The Most Dangerous Man in America?" We weren't impressed when we first heard his radio show. There seemed to be lots of sound and fury and little else. Not that we should have been surprised. After all, he'd just been a Top 40 deejay spinning records on obscure radio stations. He's a clown, we thought, an entertainer; surely not someone people would take seriously?

Then things started to happen which alarmed us. Rush's books made it on the *New York Times* Bestseller List — and on the nonfiction side! Listeners to his radio show were being counted in the millions and his TV show was an overnight success. Even worse, he began appearing on serious programs such as "Meet the Press" and "Nightline," where serious reporters asked him serious questions. Was it possible we'd been wrong? Was Rush really not dangerous?

To answer these questions, we began to monitor Rush daily. We listened to his three-hour radio show during the day. We sat through his TV show every night. We even subscribed to his newsletter, and bought and read both of his books.

The result is our newsletter, the *Flush Rush Quarterly*, and this book. Ours is a dirty job, but we couldn't come up with a better way to point out the distortions, half-truths, contradictions, and lies that flow from the Great White One.

For example, early in 1993, Rush blamed a downturn of the economy on President Clinton's proposed budget, although it hadn't yet been passed. A month later, Clinton took credit for an economic upswing, claiming it happened because people were feeling good about the budget, which still hadn't passed. Rush's reaction? He was flabbergasted: "How could Democrats take credit for this even before the budget was passed?"

Rush ridicules environmentalists and never passes up a chance to attack them as tree-huggers and wackos. At the same time, he boasts that American factories are among the cleanest in the world, failing to mention that the much despised "environmentalist wackos" are largely responsible for the august ranking.

He's quick to point out problems, real or imagined, but offers only impractical, simple solutions to complicated situations — when he bothers to offer any at all. Moral decay in this country could be halted it were more difficult to get out of marriages. (But,

then again, Rush has gotten out of two marriages himself.) The homeless would disappear overnight if they'd just get jobs. (Maybe the more ambitious among them could follow Rush's example and get a gig on the family-owned radio station.)

He has a vicious streak, too. When Kurt Cobain, lead singer of the group Nirvana, took his own life, Rush called him "human debris" and remarked that he used a shotgun so "he wouldn't miss this time." He thought it was funny when poor single moms were conned into applying for nonexistent jobs. And he finds humor in ridiculing the physical aspects of others, including the stature of Robert Reich and Janet Reno. As David Letterman said after Rush remarked that, in a photo, Hillary Rodham Clinton resembled a Pontiac hood ornament, "You can say that because you're the finest looking human specimen on this planet."

He's a man who didn't vote until he was 35 years old and yet asserts he is a super patriot. He tap-danced around the Vietnam draft yet claims to have a thorough understanding of things military, even as he criticizes President Clinton for not having served. Dangerous? Considering Rush claims to be right 99.8% of the time, and millions believe him, we think so.

We've put together a collection of quotes from Rush Limbaugh's radio show covering the period January 1993 through April 1994 and from his two books, *The Way Things Ought To Be* (New York: Pocket Books, 1992) and *See, I Told You So* (New York: Pocket Books, 1993). Rush once said, "Not once will you read a refutation of what I say or what I believe. Not once will you hear them say that what I say is incorrect or wrong and then prove it. Not once will you hear them accurately state my beliefs and then refute them."

Well, Rush is right about that. We didn't do it once. We did it dozens of times. Read on and see for yourself.

A LITTLE EDUCATION GOES A LONG WAY

Rush on pupils today:
... since when is a C– hard to maintain? When I went to school, attaining a C was considered embarrassingly average.

Rush as a pupil:
When I was in junior high school, teachers graded with Ds and Fs and, believe me, I got some.

The problem with reading books is that it takes time.

Big vocabulary, usable vocabulary; uh, the ability to speak and write properly will convince people that you're educated and smart when you might not be educated in terms of a wide breadth of knowledge.

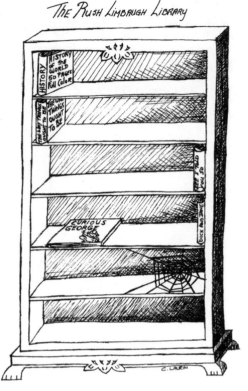

Examples of Rush's big vocabulary:

Death is, is, uh, what it is.

The reason we have crime is because we have bad guys.

Sometimes I didn't want to go to school. I skipped the entire month of April my senior year because I didn't want to go. I was just fed up with it...

The words you use tell others about your education, your background, even your intelligence.

Some insight into Rush's intelligent grasp of words:

They sold worldwide rights to my first book to Poland, England, and Japan. The book will be translated into these three languages.

I'm not going to sit here and stand for this.

I do not make *ad hominem* attacks on Clinton. They all deal with policy — or character.

Ad hominem, according to *Webster's Dictionary*, means marked by an attack on an opponent's character rather than by an answer to his contentions.

There is no such thing as an implied contract.

Yes, there is. Implied contract, according to *Barron's Law Dictionary*, is a quasi contract, obligations created by law for reasons of justice.

Don't Know Much about History ...
There are more American Indians alive today than there were when Columbus arrived or any other time in history. Does that sound like a record of genocide?

Yes, there are more American Indians alive today than in 1492 — but only 400,000 more over a span of five centuries. American Indians numbered approximately 1 million in 1492. That number fell to 237,000 in 1900. It's estimated some 1,400,000 live in the US today — largely because the white man stopped killing them about the turn of the century — with about 50% on reservations. Many tribes, including the Massachuset and Suquehannock, no longer exist.

On August 1, 1620, the Mayflower set sail. It carried a total of 102 passengers, including 40 Pilgrims led by William Bradford. On the journey, Bradford set up an agreement that established just and equal laws for all members of their community irrespective of their religious beliefs.

> **No, he didn't. The Mayflower Compact only included freedom of religion for the passengers who were either the Separatist Pilgrims or had a more favorable relationship with the Church of England. Catholics and Jews need not apply.**

It was their [the early New England Pilgrims' and the Puritans'] commitment to pluralism and free worship that led to these ideas being incorporated into American life.

> **Puritan New England was a closed society and only male members of the church were eligible to vote. These same "pluralists" martyred a few pesky Quakers and chased Roger Williams, the actual designer of "free worship," into exile in Rhode Island.**

...think back to Thomas Jefferson and Abraham Lincoln and James Madison. Can you imagine them in, in deciding whether or not to take on the British for our independence?

> **Abraham Lincoln?**

Always the opponent of government intervention in the affairs business, young Simon Legree Limbaugh was named Manager of the Year for the Pennsylvania Coal Mine Association in 1905 for getting the most productivity from the 6-to-12-year- old age group. (photo by Lewis Hine)

This brings us to our Founding Fathers — the geniuses who crafted the Declaration of Independence and the US Constitution. Don't believe the conventional wisdom of our day that claims these men were anything but orthodox, Bible-believing Christians.

> **We're not convinced Rush writes his own books, but now it seems he doesn't even read them. As he correctly points out in his first book, *The Way Things Ought To Be*, Thomas Jefferson was a deist. According to the *New Columbia Encyclopedia*, so were Washington and Franklin. Deism is an unorthodox religion that regards formal religion as superfluous and teaches that people should depend on reason rather than revelation or the teachings of any church.**

I think dinosaurs were a mistake. Whether of creation or evolution, they were a mistake and that's why they are gone.

Don't Know Much Geography ...
Since you bring up China, I wasn't gonna talk about this, but [here's] a memo to US businessmen trying to make money in Russia: You're in the wrong hemisphere. You need to head to China...

E.I.B. TATTLER 50¢

New World Order Scoop !!
Black Forest moved from Germany to Russia !!

MAP AREA ENLARGED

DETAILS PAGE A 12

Russia

C. LAURIN

The incident occurred near the Black Forest of Russia.

THE MOST DANGEROUS MAN IN AMERICA

"Do you ever wake up in the middle of the night and just think to yourself, I'm just full of hot gas?"

— David Letterman, to Rush

I seldom talk about myself.

Number of times Rush Limbaugh said I, me, myself, or Rush Limbaugh in a five-minute span, 9:09 to 9:14 am on October 27, 1993: 74

Nobody handed it to me on a silver platter. I had to work at it to prove myself every step of the way.

According to *Current Biography*, Rush's first job in radio was at a station owned by his father.

Caller: Thank you for being the voice of conservative opportunists.

Rush: You're gonna love my next book. It's right up your alley.

> **Opportunism: The practice of taking advantage of circumstances especially with little regard for principles or consequences. — *Webster's Dictionary***

I start this show at noon saying, All right, am I gonna be able to put all these random thoughts I have, am I gonna be able to ad lib them into an organized, cogent fashion? And every time I think I have, I feel better, too.

I've never been one to deal here with innuendo and to spread literal rumor ...

Oh, really?

Okay, folks. I think I got enough information here to tell you about the contents of this fax I got. Brace yourselves ... Vince Foster was murdered in an apartment owned by Hillary Clinton and the body was taken to Fort Marcy Park.

Going out on a limb:

I have other thoughts that I'm gonna wait a couple of weeks or so to mention. In fact, I'm going to wait until it happens. And I'm gonna say, "Folks, back on May 20 I was gonna predict to you something." Um, I'm not gonna actually spell out the prediction. I'm just gonna predict to you what I think is gonna happen will happen. I'm right about it now and you'll just have to trust me. When it does happen, when I tell you, "Yep, this is what I meant when I predicted it on May 20, but didn't specify," this is what I meant.

Commenting on a critical article in the *Washington Post*:
Why now? Why is all of this coming out now? ... This is not conspiratorial. I don't want the press saying, "Here's Limbaugh fearing these conspiracies again." No, no, no. I'm not fearing conspiracies.

Ten minutes later:
This story in the *Washington Post* yesterday was written by a guy who used to be a Moscow correspondent for the *Washington Post*. Now he's a staff writer for the *New Yorker*, which is where Sydney Blumenthal is, who hates this show and is a big fan of Hillary. So there is a connection ...

Rush in his December 1993 interview with *Playboy*:
Nice guys never get laid.

Rush later assuages the fears of his religious-right followers:
I didn't talk about anything sexual with *Playboy*.

Asked if he was worried about an upcoming biography, Rush replied:
No. I've never gotten anybody pregnant. Only smoked marijuana two times. Never did drugs.

The crowd wanting to legalize drugs are made up of two things. One, selfishness. Uh, I forgot the second thing.

Warning: The Surgeon General reports marijuana use causes loss of memory.

Garth W. Limbaugh, with his friend Wayne, experiments with marijuana in the early 1600s during a "Say No to Drugs" meeting. After The Smoker by Adrian Brouwer, 1605-1638.

After playing a tape of Senator Moynihan, who stuttered once or twice talking about increasing the tax on bullets:
Obviously the major problem is not guns. It's alcoholism.

And Rush demonstrating his own flawless speaking skills:
Okay, okay. All right. Ah, I'm saying, uh, I'm, uh, uh. It could well be ah, ah, ah; if it's this, if it's that bad, it's worse than I thought. I'm, I'm open to this.

I would do anything to help out the military.

How about enlist? Consider ...
I had student deferments in college and, upon taking a physical, was discovered to have a physical — uh, by virtue of what the military says; I didn't even know it existed — a physical deferment. And then the lottery system came along — when they choose your lot by your birthdate, and mine was high.
And I didn't want to go. Just as Governor Clinton didn't.

One year later:
I did not get a medical deferment. I had student deferments.

On the other hand:
Never trust a draft dodger.

Look, I don't doubt that, as a human being, Bill Clinton cares for people. I don't know too many human beings who are so devoid of feeling that they are ambivalent or apathetic about people and their plight.

But later:
It's just one of those human emotions that I have a problem with. I have a problem being sympathetic. I can say it like I believe it, but I don't have a lot of sympathy.

> **"There are broader audiences to be reached because our orange juice leaves a good taste with people and should be promoted on programs with good taste."**
> — Florida Governor Lawton Chiles, on the Florida Citrus Commission's decision to advertise on Rush's radio show

What I find especially appalling is that so many people seem happy that misery persists, because it enables them to say, "I told you so."

> So wrote Rush in his first book, *The Way Things Ought To Be.* What was the name of his second book? *See, I Told You So.*

I think it is dangerous when bad taste is championed as a "must permit" under the First Amendment ... And I am alarmed that those who are the purveyors of lewdness, sickness, and all that are somehow being defended under these auspices.

Rush purveys Bad Taste, Lewdness, and Sickness: [Reagan] must have been having anal intercourse with all the people in the country who have AIDS because AIDS activists say Ronald Reagan is responsible for that, too.

Remember, most men would not sleep with Madonna ... I mean, it's taking your life into your hands. Who knows the area you're gonna be visiting? Where it's been? And who has been, you know, a recent visitor? You never know with somebody like that.

Caller, discussing the rape of a 79-year-old woman: How can you possibly rape someone without premeditating it?
Rush: Irresistible impulse?

She really licked her!
> Said after some elections results from the National Organization for Women were announced on his television show.

I'm just trying to get people to open their minds and think like I do...

I always try to pull myself out of myself and get an objective perspective.

Here are a few examples of Rush's objectivity. First of all, on his second book, *See, I Told You So*:

I'm telling you, we have another Bible coming here, folks!

Caller: You can't take every issue and stand staunchly on one side just because you are conservative.
Rush: You can. You must. That's called principle.
Caller: What if your principles are wrong?
Rush: They're not. That's not a concern of mine.

... this is not bragging ... this show is ridiculed by too many people who don't listen to it as being reactionary nonsense. And this show is not. This show is extremely contributory. And since no one will judge it that way, we must.

Let me take what you said and illustrate something else.

We are kind and patient, tolerant and compassionate with all first-time callers.

But, afterwards:
Richard, this is my show! You're making wild-assed, stupid, indefensible accusations and you're damn lucky I put you on the air to talk about it in the first place!

I used to watch "Superman" all the time. And I had a Superman suit. I was asking my mom to buy Superman suits all the time because I could never get one to fit and look like it did on TV.

"In the end, Limbaugh is a man who thrives on intellectual masturbation and then brags about how well he makes love."
— Stephen W. Bell,
Buffalo News

"I'm amazed that somebody named Rush would have such a slow metabolism."
— Dennis Miller

Question: What's the difference between Rush Limbaugh and a whale?
Answer: Fifty pounds and a sports jacket

RUSH'S VIEW OF THE WORLD

"The world does not revolve around Limbaugh, although he is large enough."

– Spokesperson for
Congressman John Dingell

I view what I'm doing here as the epitome of positive. I am doing what I think is the ultimate in positive.

Rush accentuates the positive: We are in a race between civilization and catastrophe. We have record murder and violent crime rates, huge increases in births to unwed mothers, education decline, broken families...

We're in big trouble out there, folks. I think the country may be finished.

I think that we have so many bitter, angry people in charge of the way we educate our kids in America ...

Ask yourself why the morale in the military is so low. And it clearly is.

Love is the only human emotion you can't control; you can't fake it. Except women — and thank God.

Marriage has been devalued in this country at every turn ... People get married with the notion it will be easy to get out of it if it doesn't work out.

> **How many times has Rush Limbaugh gotten out of a marriage? Twice.**

When you think of the things that give you your best memories, they have nothing to do with money. They all have to do with the relationships you have with people — your friends, your family, the people you love. Those are the things that give you the substance and meaning in your life.

> **But later (presumably after his mother left the building):** A man's contentment and happiness is [sic] first determined by his perception of career. It's in the genes. If we asked men what's most important to you, does anybody think 7 of 10 men will say their relationship? No! It won't happen unless there is a wife or woman nearby who wants you to say it.

True, there are many misunderstandings and much anger about AIDS, but don't let those emotions prevent you from offering what these people need most: your support and love.

> **Rush on AIDS activists, though:**
> Get out of our schools, get out of our churches. Take your deadly, sickly behavior and keep it to yourselves.

You are wise to understand what happens when a journalist doesn't challenge an idiotic assertion and, therefore, the idiotic assertion is left to stand even though half of the people who hear it are scratching their heads.

Just a few of Rush's idiotic assertions:
It's the vanity of humanity to think we can warm the earth at all.

Columbus saved the Indians from themselves.

I am convinced that 1.3 million or 1.5 million abortions per year since 1973 has [sic] been a primary contributor to the overall lack of respect for life we have in this country and the rising crime rate and the rising illegitimacy rate.

My job is to rewrite the truth about Ronald Reagan.

Ronald Reagan was the greatest president of the twentieth century.

A survey of 750 historians chosen at random from a list kept by the American Historical Association showed that nine out of ten respondents considered Reagan intellectually unqualified to be president. Only 1% ranked him "great."

The Creation of
Ignorance. After a detail
in the Sistine Chapel by
Michelangelo, 1475-1564.

Character matters! How can you trust anybody's opinions on the issues if you can't trust them. If you have questions about their veracity and honesty, what difference does what they say about anything make?

Someone who disregards the Constitution is a dangerous radical.

And yet ...

This [Star Wars] was war. Cold war. [Reagan] faked them out! And in the process, we faked out our own Congress and we did it! It's okay to lie to Congress because they lie to us!

And as Oliver North admitted, upon being asked who made him lie during the Iran-Contra scandal: "Well, the President of the United States."

While we're on the subject of Iran-Contra:

They wanted to find illegal activity on anybody in the Reagan Administration. They couldn't find any. These guys didn't do anything. There was no evidence, not one indictment, not one charge.

Robert McFarlane: National Security Advisor in the Reagan White House pleaded guilty to four misdemeanor counts of withholding from Congress information about the Administration's efforts to help the Contras.

Lt. Col. Oliver North: former National Security Council aide was convicted of obstructing Congress, destroying documents, and accepting illegal gratuities. These convictions were later overturned because immunized evidence before Congress was used at his trial.

Richard V. Secord: a retired Air Force major general plead guilty to making a false statement to Congress.

John Poindexter: succeeded Robert McFarlane as National Security Advisor; convicted of conspiracy to mislead Congress, obstructing Congressional inquiries, and making false statements to the House.

Alan D. Fiers: former chief of the CIA's Latin America task force pleaded guilty to withholding information from Congress.

Clair E. George: former chief of Covert Operations for the CIA was convicted of lying to Congress.

Elliot L. Abrams: former Assistant Secretary of State pleaded guilty to withholding information from Congress.

Duane R. Clarridge: former chief of Operations for the CIA was indicted on perjury charges.

Caspar Weinberger: former Secretary of Defense was indicted on charges of lying to Congress.

George Bush: President of the United States pardoned McFarlane, Fiers, George, Abrams, Clarridge, and Weinberger on Christmas Eve 1992.

Ronald Reagan cut everything in the budget, and yet they say he made the biggest deficit in the country. I don't know how they come up with that. It's Washington math.

> **Ronald Reagan did not cut everything in the budget. For example, according to the U.S. Office of Management and Budget, defense spending reached an all-time high during his administration—a total of $2,183,170,000,000.00 And the deficit increased an unprecedented $1,615,290,000,000.00.**

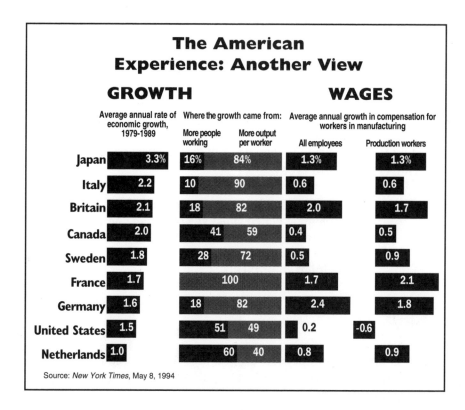

The American Experience: Another View

GROWTH

WAGES

	Average annual rate of economic growth, 1979-1989	Where the growth came from:		Average annual growth in compensation for workers in manufacturing	
		More people working	More output per worker	All employees	Production workers
Japan	3.3%	16%	84%	1.3%	1.3%
Italy	2.2	10	90	0.6	0.6
Britain	2.1	18	82	2.0	1.7
Canada	2.0	41	59	0.4	0.5
Sweden	1.8	28	72	0.5	0.9
France	1.7	100		1.7	2.1
Germany	1.6	18	82	2.4	1.8
United States	1.5	51	49	0.2	-0.6
Netherlands	1.0	60	40	0.8	0.9

Source: *New York Times*, May 8, 1994

From 1982 through 1990, the United States experienced 96 continuous months of economic growth — the longest in peacetime history. Did I already say that? Good. It needs to be repeated and repeated to counter the lies.

> **Rush, please see the table above, based, with kind permission, on one in the *New York Times*, May 8, 1994.**
> **And what would have happened if we hadn't, as Lloyd Bentsen, Secretary of the Treasury, has said, been writing "two trillion dollars in hot checks?"**

People say I never have solutions to problems. Well, I'm going to give you two solutions to solving the deficit problem. And then I'll show you why these two ways won't work.

Ronald Reagan is a man who we Americans owe a debt that we will never be able to repay.

> **When Ronald Reagan entered the White House, the federal budget deficit stood at $74 billion and the national debt at $1 trillion. By 1992, the debt had risen to $4 trillion and cost the taxpayers about $235 billion a year in interest payments.**

Federal spending on poverty programs in 1991 dollars increased from $140 billion in 1982 to $180 billion in 1991, an annual growth of 3%.

% of Children below Poverty Level

	1980	1990
All races	17.9	19.9
White	13.4	15.1
Black	42.1	44.2
Hispanic	33	39.7
(US Bureau of Census)		

The top 1% paid more than 25% of all federal income taxes in 1990, a 40% increase over 1980, according to the Congressional Budget Office. The bottom 60% paid 11% of federal taxes in 1990, 20% less than in 1980.

But then, the top 1% also owned over one-third of the wealth. Moreover, the *Economist* reported on January 20, 1990, that "in the 1980s, median family income stagnated, the number of millionaires trebled, and that of billionaires quintupled. The rich provided an increasing proportion of the tax take; but the effective tax rates for the poor rose, while those for the rich fell."

... people are responding to what I say because it is right. My wit and wisdom are like a lifeline of reason tossed to a culture nearly drowning in confusion and murkiness.

How's this for confusion and murkiness?
And on "Meet the Press" yesterday, see, you can't have it both ways. You cannot have Ronald Reagan as raising taxes more than anyone in history and at the same time cutting taxes so much that the deficit and all these economic corrections we have make, ah, take place — or the economic mistake causing the corrections took place.

I'm just trying to prevent a rewrite of history, ah, as to passing judgement on the '82 tax increase. Look, let's be honest. It was a Bob Dole-led deal.

Interest rates were brought down from the stratosphere. The stock market nearly tripled in value. America reached full employment while simultaneously nullifying ... inflation ...

> "Once you correct for the ups and downs of the business cycle, the growth path of the economy was virtually the same before and after Reagan took office. Through all the Reagan years, productivity rose on average less than 1% annually." — Paul Krugman, *Peddling Prosperity* (New York: W. W. Norton & Co., 1994)

Average real family income grew by well over 15% from 1982 to 1989, according to the Bureau of Census.

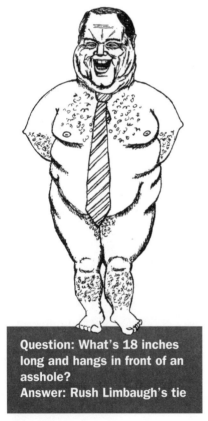

Question: What's 18 inches long and hangs in front of an asshole?
Answer: Rush Limbaugh's tie

The reason average income increased is because the rich got richer. A more telling statistic is that relating to median income. Just a reminder from your arithmetic class: Average income is the total income of all families in the nation, divided by the total number of families. Median income is reckoned by listing all incomes separately and then choosing the income which falls in the middle of that list. So median income is a better reflection of how the "average" family is doing.

Seen here with the nation's business leaders in 1900, Cornelius Vanderbilt Limbaugh commited a major faux pas by eating the laurel wreath as an appetizer instead of wearing it on his head as was the tradition. (Photo by Percy Byron)

"In this country, free market purists, like TV preachers, can denounce the system for not living up to their principles while remaining secure in the assumption that they will never have to live under a system that does, or that expects them to. In a society of minimal government — the Wild West, say — Limbaugh would be a fat boy who dances when you shoot at his feet."
— Roy Blount, Jr.

Working people today are more frustrated than ever before because they have less buying power. Why do they have less buying power? Because they are being taxed into serfdom. Americans now work an average of 123 days to pay their tax bills at the federal, state, and local levels. That's not free enterprise, my friends, that's slavery.

We hate to bring up the debt again, but ... About half the days we spend working to pay our federal income taxes go towards servicing the interest on the debt and the savings and loan bailout.

If you choose to believe this class warfare propaganda that the S&L was nothing but a bailout for the rich, think about this. Who invested in the S&Ls? You. Individual people.... If you're tired of bailing out the S&Ls, then send back the money that you've got. Let's be honest here.

"High-flying speculators did not take long to realize that owning an S&L was a key to the Treasury. The S&Ls were an invitation to gamble with someone else's money — the taxpayers' of the United States." — L. William Seidman, former head of the FDIC (Federal Deposit Insurance Corporation) in the Reagan and Bush administrations, in his book *Full Faith and Credit* (New York: Random House, 1993).

It was in this so-called "Decade of Greed" that Americans became more charitable than ever before ... the 1980s were, indeed, the Decade of Giving ... the annual rate of growth in total giving in the 1980s was nearly 55% higher than in the previous 25 years ...

But who was giving? According to Kevin Phillips's book *Boiling Point* (New York: Random House, 1993) between 1980 and 1988 taxpayers with incomes over $1 million reduced their charitable contributions from $207,089 to $72,784 and those in the $500,000-to-$1 million bracket $47,432 to $16,602. On the other hand, those with incomes between $25,000 and $30,000 upped their average donations by 62%.

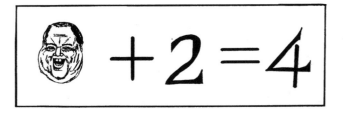

I'm the fourth branch of government. Why am I the fourth branch of government? Because the other two let it happen.

Oh, give me an example of when I paint with too broad of a brush.

Conservatives are pretty much self-sufficient, self-reliant. They will take care of their own and it's up to you to take care of yours. Liberals think that nobody is capable of taking care of themselves and have to be taken care of. And they look to government as a way to right the wrongs of society. I may be making this a bit complicated.

I mean, I probably more accurately present the liberal side of things than they do!

We don't think so ...

The way females seek to advance themselves if they are feminists is to prove they've been victimized and they want to ask a court or some other agency to leapfrog them beyond their current position without having earned it legitimately.

Typical liberal approach ... It's like, if we just get rid of our nukes, maybe they wouldn't nuke us.

What do we know about American liberals? American liberals decry the military, period. The military is the focus of evil. If the military didn't exist, then the rest of the world wouldn't feel threatened.

Liberalism thinks nothing of average people. You're incapable, incompetent, you're idiotic, you cannot read. That's what they think.

We [conservatives] do not want to become people who can only defeat our political opposition by virtue of scandalizing what they do.

Two minutes later ...

What this [Whitewater] offers is a great weapon to attack the credibility and veracity of these people so that the next time it is that they run for something, or they support somebody running for something, or they support a plan that they claim is this or that, it will be easier to assail their motives and their plan.

On the 1992 presidential elections, in which he backed the losing candidate (from Paul D. Colford, *The Rush Limbaugh Story*, New York: St Martin's Press, 1993):

I was not wrong about anything. I was not wrong about why people voted the way they did. I was not wrong about what people are expecting. I was not wrong — I did blow the prediction [a Bush victory by four to six points]. I did blow the prediction, but let's be honest: I was simply remaining true to my cause.

Those of you who want to take off the Clinton/Gore bumper stickers, just go get a handicapped parking sticker instead, and people will know why you voted that way.

We're not altogether surprised Rush has such contempt for the popular vote. This is, after all, a man who didn't register to vote until he was 35.

Rush reviews President Clinton's cabinet appointments: We've had three attorneys general; we've had three secretaries of defense; two communications directors. Look at the Surgeon General! I mean, it's an embarrassment. I mean, it's an absolute embarrassment!

> **Here's a quick review of some of Ronald Reagan's first-term appointments: six high officials were indicted and 25 were fired, or forced to resign, or forced to withdraw their nominations because of ethics charges.**

In the late 1930s, America was looking at a 22% unemployment rate. There was no such concept as welfare. There was no minimum wage guarantee. There was no "safety net" except the one that family members provided.

> **During the Depression, state and local agencies and charities handled welfare. In 1938, the Fair Labor Standards Act set a minimum wage. The federally funded Civilian Conservation Corps employed about two and a half million men and the Civil Works Administration put to work another four million.**

Somebody show me where in history giving tax breaks made somebody wealthy.

> **Headline in the *Los Angeles Times* the very same day: "Developers get $366 million tax break in budget bill."**

I know families that make $180,000 a year and they don't consider themselves rich. Why, it costs $20,000 a year to send their kids to college.

> **Then again:** $14,400 for a family of four? That's not so bad.

Do you think Bill Clinton has ever read John Adams?

> **Rush, have you? That's the Federalist president who, in 1798, signed into law the Sedition Act which threatened with fines or imprisonment anyone who "shall write, print, utter, or publish ... scandalous and malicious writing or writings against the government of the United States, or either the Congress ... or the President ... with intent to defame ... or to bring them ... into contempt or disrepute."**

Big labor is against [NAFTA, the North American Free Trade Agreement], so for that reason alone, I'm for it.

Let me tell you what jobs are going south with NAFTA.

If you are unskilled and uneducated, your job is going south. Skilled workers, educated people are going to do just fine 'cause those are the kinds of jobs NAFTA is going to create.

If we are going to start rewarding no skills and stupid people, I'm serious: let unskilled jobs, the kind of jobs that take absolutely no knowledge whatsoever to do, let stupid and unskilled Mexicans do that work.

> **Of President Clinton's plan to revamp the federal student loan program to save money currently paid to banks, Rush said:**

The banks are taking all the risks in issuing the loans, so they are entitled to the profits.

> **Banks take no risks at all since these loans are federally insured. If a student defaults, a guarantor agency repays the lender then collects the amount owed. If that agency is unsuccessful, the government pays off the loan.**

On possible US intervention in Bosnia:
It's amazing to me that we have to go around the world because people are dying.

Responding to a critic:
You're saying because I didn't serve — this is the age-old argument — I didn't serve, therefore I'm not qualified to have credibility on the importance of national defense.

But, later:
[Clinton] wants to lead the American military, a man who says he's qualified to do so because he called out the Arkansas National Guard a couple of times.

Commenting on the Gulf War:
Everybody in the world was aligned with the US except who? The United States Congress.

> **Wrong. Both the United States Senate and the House of Representatives approved the use of force against Iraq in the Persian Gulf.**

Time is doing a piece on people who despise Clinton and they want a quote from me ... Have they ever listened to this show? Have they ever heard anything that would indicate we despise him personally?

But earlier:
Have you forgotten how the actions of Bill Clinton probably have resulted in the deaths of more prisoners of war in Vietnam because it gave aid and comfort to the North Vietnamese? ... If you think he was actively working for the defeat of the United States and the death of US soldiers, then he is even more diabolical than I think. And it may well be ...

We don't need national health insurance and socialized medicine, Hillary. I have the cure for what ails us. Here's my prescription: Self-reliance. Morality. Personal responsibility. Optimism and good cheer. Confidence in the irrepressibility of the human spirit.

In fact, the health care system in this country is the envy of the world.

In fact, let's look at some numbers recently released by *Health* magazine and reproduced by kind permission:

	GERMANY	JAPAN	CANADA	BRITAIN	U.S.
Percent of population uninsured at some point in a year	1	1	1	1	26
Per capita spending on health, 1990	$1,287	$1,035	$1,795	$920	$2,566
Percent of GNP spent on health, 1991	8.5	6.5	10	5.4	13.4
Annual doctor visits per capita	11.5	12.8	6.6	6	5.3
Infant mortality per thousand	7.6	4.8	7.2	6.6	10
Percent saying system needs to be fundamentally changed, rebuilt	48	53	43	NA	89

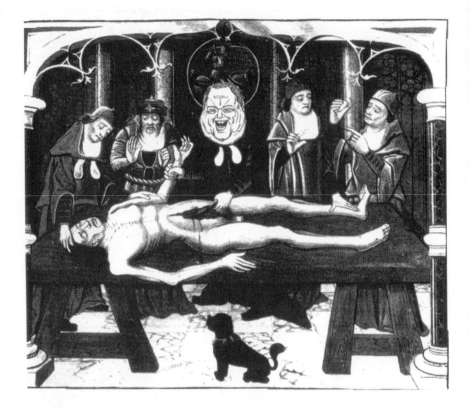

Always the prankster, Gilles de Rais
Limbaugh, the town butcher, often
disguised himself as a physician and
performed unnecessary surgery at the
local free clinic, with his four-legged
friend, Bennett, at his side. Fifteenth
century.

On National Depression Screening Day, to promote awareness of a condition that afflicts 23% of Americans between the ages of 15 and 54:

Be on the lookout! It's another manufactured crisis.

Rush's idea of a crisis:
I moved to New York and I didn't have a doctor ... I went to the emergency room to have ear wax removed ...

We want to defeat the concept of universal coverage. And the reason we want to is for social and moral reasons.

> **"Rush Limbaugh has this great racket going where he says whatever he wants to say regardless of the facts because it makes the news and it is controversial and he makes a lot of money."**
> — Hillary Rodham Clinton

> **"When I heard the results, I thought, what a shame Dr. Kevorkian doesn't do dental work."**
> — Nick Meglin, co-editor of *Mad Magazine*, learning that his readers had just selected Rush the celebrity upon whom they'd most like to perform unnecessary root-canal work.

> **"Rush is extremely sophisticated, extremely smart. He knows how to frame an issue, how to debate an issue. He's very serious intellectually."**
> — William J. Bennett, Secretary of Education under Ronald Reagan and author of *The Book of Values*

There were no public schools ... Why were people better educated before the American revolution with no public spending than in 1993 ...

The Boston Latin School opened in 1635 as the first public school in the colonies. In 1647, the Massachusetts General Court enacted legislation to appoint one teacher for every 50 households and to set up a grammar school for any town with 100 families or more. In Connecticut, the code of 1650 also required a town of 50 families to employ a teacher and a town of 100 families to operate a grammar school. All were supported with tax dollars.

... those people defining sexual harassment in grade school and so forth, you have to understand these [are] people who are angry and bitter and do not like other people and are seeking their revenge for whatever misery they feel and trying to spread it around to everybody.

Note who does the
rioting: it's the lawless

Responding to Janet Reno's testimony that as Attorney General her priority would be to protect the rights of the accused:

What about the victims? What about the rights of the law-abiding? Who cares about the criminals?

Several months later, on the subject of the rights of the accused; in this instance, the four police officers being retried for beating Rodney King:

What about double jeopardy? Self-incrimination? What about the officers' fifth amendment rights?

Commenting on the riots that erupted in Montreal after its hockey team won the Stanley Cup:

You know what could have stopped this? Richard Daley in 1968 in the Democratic National Convention issued an order — when there were rumors of riots — he issued a shoot-to-kill order. And there were no riots; there was no civil disobedience; and no shots were fired; and nobody was hurt. And that's what ought to happen.

Mayor Daly's order was issued not at the Democratic Convention, but following the assassination of Martin Luther King, Jr., on April 4, 1968. Four months later, protestors flocked to the Democratic Convention and engaged in some of the most riotous civil disobedience in the history of the United States.

There's an ozone hole, all right. But it's a hole in the theory, not in the sky.

> "Already there is evidence that some particularly vulnerable animal species, including frogs, may be adversely affected by an increase in ultraviolet radiation. As for humans, skin cancer cases increase in direct proportion to distance from the equator ... Today there is less stratospheric ozone than ever recorded in fifteen years of measurement ..."
> — *New York Times*, March 20, 1994

There is no global warming. In fact, it's getting cooler.

Note: This comment was made in early October.

Could anybody show me a dolphin that's ever built a hospital or a highway or invented an automobile?

"The most beautiful thing about a tree is what you do with it when you kill it" was first said by Paul Bunyan Limbaugh. Soon after this picture was taken, Paul Limbaugh died a tragic death by choking on some shell in a spotted owl-egg omelette. After a photograph by Darius Kinsey.

The most beautiful thing about a tree is what you do with it when you kill it.

> Rush, do you remember Dixy Lee Ray's book, *Environmental Overkill* (Washington, DC: Regnery Gateway, 1993)? That's the one about which you said, "A way must be found to get this book into the hands of as many Americans as possible."
>
> We'd like to remind you of a passage in it: "Isn't there some additional way of improving urban air quality without all the new, expensive regulations? Indeed there is — by using the same phenomenon that nature does: photosynthesis. By planting lots of green growing plants downtown, we could bring to cities a breath of fresh air."
>
> Rush, when you plant a tree in memory of Dixy Lee Ray, we will hug it for you!

Oh, this is music to my ears when another tree bites the dust and, once again, something beautiful results — a baseball bat, the piano, and maybe even a home; the barrel, uh, rather, the handle of a rifle.

Environmentalists want forests to stay so they can grow pot without detection.

Panic, fear, dread, doom and gloom — that's what the environmental movement is all about ... Do the following ecohysterics sound familiar?

• In ten years, city dwellers will need gas masks to breathe.

• In a decade, America's mighty rivers will have reached boiling point.

• In ten years, all important animal life in the sea will be extinct. Large areas of coastline will have to be evacuated because of the stench of dead fish.

• Five years is all we have left if we are going to preserve any kind of world.

We hear wild claims like this every day from environmental wackos, right? Trouble is, these notable predictions weren't made last week or last month or even last year. All of them were made more than 20 years ago ... on or before the very first Earth Day in 1970!

> Now, Rush, we're willing to concede that these predictions may seem somewhat extreme with hindsight. But may we just refer you to some of the environmental laws that have been effected since 1970, when the Environmental Protection Agency was established, to help prevent them from coming true: the Clean Air Act (1970), the Water Pollution Control Act (1972), the Toxic Substances Control Act (1976), the National Forest Management Act (1976), and the Clean Air Act amendments (1977). Even your friend Dixy Lee noted, "There has been considerable progress. And for that we can be thankful ..."

The spotted owl is not smart enough to appreciate us saving it.

If the spotted owl can't adjust to the timber industry, then screw it!

If you put the population of the world, which you could do, inside a geographic area the size of Texas, and put them in the United States, where capitalism reigns, there would be no starvation.

We moved the recycle box out of our office to make room for the popcorn popper.

Rush: I would maintain to you we are not fragily [sic] balanced ecologically. I think it's a vanity to suggest that mankind can destroy the world.
Caller: Oh, I think the world will be here. I'm just not sure it would be the kind of world you and I would enjoy living in.

FEMINAZIS, MULTICULTURALIST PIGS, AND UGLO-AMERICANS

"There's a new organization being formed. It's called Feminists, Homeless, and Blacks for Limbaugh. And they're meeting in a phone booth in Wichita."
— Larry King

"Being attacked by Rush Limbaugh is like being gummed by a newt."
— Molly Ivins

I'm a nice guy, a harmless little fuzzball with a strong live and let live credo.

("I'm just a harmless little fuzzball," said a man arrested for threatening the life of President Clinton. "I like Rush, I sure do.")

Liberals have to stoop to name-calling because their arguments lack substance.

Rush stoops. Try to match his name-calling with his target. (The answers are upside down at the bottom of the page.)

Feminazi	People for the Ethical Treatment of Animals [PETA]
Smut Queen	Warren Christopher
Little Hand Grenade with a Bad Haircut	Jesse Jackson
Animal Rights Idiots	Democrats
Environmental Wackos	Bill Clinton
Blithering Jewel of Colossal Ignorance	Socialists
Slime, Stupid, Morons	Baby Boomers
Totally Brainless Ditz	Educators
Prune Face	Ross Perot
Racist	Greenpeace
Long-haired Maggot-Infested FM Radio Types	Sally Kirkland
Commie Libs	Anti-War Activists
Slick Willie	Madonna
Multiculturalist Pigs	National Organization for Women [NOW]
Little Coward	Robert Reich
Human Debris	Carol Moseley Braun

Feminazi = NOW; Smut Queen = Madonna; Little Hand Grenade = Ross Perot; Animal Rights Idiots = PETA; Environmental Wackos = Greenpeace; Blithering Jewel of Colossal Ignorance = Carol Moseley Braun; Slime, Stupid, Morons = Democrats; Totally Brainless Ditz = Sally Kirkland; Prune Face = Warren Christopher; Racist = Jesse Jackson; Long-Haired Maggot-Infested FM Radio Types = Anti-War Activists; Commie Libs = Socialists; Slick Willie = Bill Clinton; Multiculturalist Pigs = Educators; Little Coward = Robert Reich; Human Debris = Baby Boomers

Who said the 60's kids looked good and smelled good? ... not all of them smelled good. If you were at Woodstock, you would know what I mean. And I wasn't there. But I saw pictures.

I didn't wear blue jeans back then because I didn't want to be identified with the anti-war crowd.

> **Was this a political statement, a fashion statement, or just that he couldn't find a pair in his size?**

See, women who don't find me attractive have to be lesbians or feminists.

When it is good-looking studs, keep women off juries. It's one of the things I've been on the cutting edge of...

The Menendez brothers are some of the biggest skunk liars in the world. Who believed them? Who believed them?! A bunch of suburban liberal women just bought into everything these guys said.

> **This was but a single moment in a week-long attack on women jurors, based on the outcome of the Erik Menendez trial. Rush didn't mention the other half of the story, the guilty verdicts in Erik's brother, Lyle's, trial:**

> **Killing of Jose Menendez**
> | | |
> |---|---|
> | **First-degree murder:** | 2 women, 1 man |
> | **Second-degree murder:** | 2 women, 1 man |
> | **Voluntary Manslaughter:** | 3 women, 3 men |

> **Killing of Kitty Menendez**
> | | |
> |---|---|
> | **First-degree murder:** | 2 women, 1 man |
> | **Second-degree murder:** | 2 women, 1 man |
> | **Voluntary manslaughter:** | 2 women, 3 men |

> | | |
> |---|---|
> | **Involuntary manslaughter:** | 1 woman |

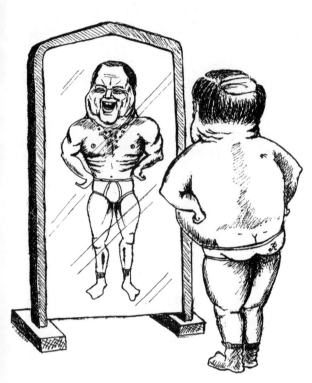

When I said women shouldn't have the right to vote, I was just being funny.

But, earlier:
If you're going to be funny, you have to have truth rooted in your effort.

Those [feminist] women don't understand the animal attractiveness that Joey Buttafuoco represents to most people in this country.

All women think they are fat.

If you can talk to her and change her mind, then she is reasonable.

Feminism was established to allow unattractive women easier access to the mainstream of society.

Rush math:
Seventy-two percent of all high school seniors say they've had sexual intercourse. Eighty-two percent of high school senior girls say have have been sexually harassed. Do you believe that? What that means is if 82% of high school female seniors say they have been harassed, uh, it means that having sex is harassment.

Rush logic:
If she calls you sweetie, it's an invitation.

Rush exposition:
Today's feminists are confusing advances with harassment; and confusing harassment with rape.

I love the women's movement. Especially when I'm walking behind it.

What the feminist movement is all about is changing basic human nature.

Women were doing quite well in this country before feminism came along.

We're in bad shape in this country when you can't look at a couple of huge knockers and notice them.

"It may sound astonishing to the young people here to know that as late as the 1970s, women could be given fewer benefits than men, denied the right to control an estate, or fired from jobs when they became pregnant."
— Ruth Bader Ginsberg, Supreme Court Justice

**Responding to a caller who claimed she was fired
because she was listening to Rush's radio show:**

Rush: I know the kind of woman who fired you. They are
humorless, they are sourpusses. They are bitter and they go
through life basically angry at the world.

Caller: Actually, she had a real good, fun personality.

All those feminazis out there demanding their right to an
abortion as the most important thing in their life never have to
worry about having one because who'd want to have sex
with 'em?

On Anita Hill:

My guess is she's [Anita Hill's] had plenty of spankings, if you
catch my meaning.

On Senator Bob Packwood:

What's the big deal? He's clumsy with women.

**And on the subject of abortion, Rush expresses his views
on "Donahue," December 24, 1993:**

Audience member: If you have a daughter ... and she was raped
... would you allow her to have an abortion?

Rush: Here's what I would do if it were my wife, if it were my
daughter. In case of rape, leave it totally up to her.

Phil Donahue: You can't. If you do, you are like Vice-President
Dan Quayle. You have a mutually irreconcilable position here.
You are not being consistent or honest with yourself when you
say that.

Rush: Phil, I was just trying to be a good liberal with my answer
and it didn't work. Here's the answer to the question. In a
situation of any kind of abortion — if I'm to be consistent — the
baby is innocent and must be born.

As a child, Clarence T. Limbaugh, later to become an important judge at the Royal Court, had many problems keeping nannies. After the Niccolini-Cowper Madonna by Raphael, 1483-1520.

Commenting on the ruling of the Supreme Court that RICO (the Racketeering Investigation Corruption Organization) Act can be used against anti-choice protestors:

The only thing about this that is in any way, shape, matter, or form pleasing is that somebody can now turn around and use it on Act Up. Somebody can now turn around and use it on Greenpeace and all the other left-wing protestors. I mean, there are actually people who go out there and destroy property in their protests and shut down businesses and so forth, far in excess of anything Operation Rescue has ever done.

"If Rush Limbaugh ever met the Pope, they wouldn't be talking about food. They would be talking about pointy white hats."
— Bobcat Goldthwait

According to the National Abortion Federation in Washington, DC, incidents of violence and disruption towards abortion providers in the US reported between 1984 and 1993 by all anti-choice organizations comprise:

Murder	1
Attempted Murder	1
Bombing	37
Arson	86
Invasion	338
Vandalism	506
Death Threats	154
Assault	66
Burglary	29
Stalking	144
Bomb Threats	290
Hate Mail and Harassing Phone Calls	1076

In addition, the total financial damage to clinics for the eleven months January to November 1993 was $3,731,529.50.

I am not a racist!

Caller: Blacks have to be heard.
Rush: Why ...? They are 12% of the population. Who the hell cares?

Question: What's the difference between Rush Limbaugh and the Hindenberg?
Answer: One is a flaming fascist gasbag, while the other is just a dirigible.

To whatever extent this nation is racist, that racism is fueled primarily by the rantings and ravings and inconsistencies, the absolute idiocies of people like Jesse Jackson and Benjamin Chavis.

> **Compare the following. First, Rush on the Martin Luther King, Jr., March on Washington, DC:**

... the NAACP should have riot rehearsal. They should get a liquor store and practice robberies.

I have a better recipe for blacks' escape from misery than the civil rights leadership does: You make black people listen to this show every day.

Now, the black population in this country is sixteen million. Twelve to sixteen million. Of that, what percentage is adult? Let's just say half. So we have two million of eight million college-educated black adults. That's a pretty good percentage compared to what you probably think.

> **According to the US Bureau of Census, the black population is over thirty million, seventeen million of whom are over 25. Yes, two million have college degrees. But that makes a percentage of only 11.7%. That's just over half the percentage of whites with college degrees and nothing like the 25% Rush imagines.**

> **Rush responds to Spike Lee's idea that black students skip school to see his movie *Malcolm X*:**

Hey, Spike! Why don't you just, why don't you close the loop? As long as you're going to tell them to skip school and go see your movie, why don't you tell them to loot the concessions stand and blow up the theater on the way out in the big spirit of Malcolm the Tenth?

If you want to reside in the black experience or the Asian experience, fine. Relegate yourself to second-class status.

Aristotle Limbaughopolous out for a run
with some friends. Seldom talked about at
Limbaugh family gatherings, Aristotle is
said to be the last Limbaugh to be physically
and intellectually fit. After a painting by
Gerhardt Heilmann.

They [Native Americans] were meaner to themselves than anybody was ever mean to them. These people were savages ... These people were out there destroying timber. They were out there conquering land. Killing each other. Scalping each other.

Rush, we're touched and surprised by your sympathy for the trees.

This is asinine! A César Chávez Day in California?

"May the commitment to the social doctrine of the Church which characterized the life and service of Mr. Chávez continue to inspire the members of the UFW in peaceful efforts to insure justice for all people."
—Pope John Paul II

There is racism in this country, but it is not as bad as people think.

When a gay person turns his back on you, it is anything but an insult. It's an invitation.

Every man would like to be in Clint Eastwood's jeans.

Female caller to Rush's radio show: I do not mentally undress men.
Rush: Oh, come on! Everyone does.

THE DITTOHEADS

"The last time this many conservatives gathered in one place was Berlin in 1935."

— Jay Leno, referring to the twenty thousand Dittoheads who showed up at Dan's Bake Sale, a publicity stunt organized by Rush. (It should be noted that Rush was offended by this insensitive joke and Leno later called to apologize to him.)

Go out and find some more calls from people who idolize me, Bo.

I truly believe, my friends, that my success is due to all of you in my audience — who I will never take for granted.

Oh, really?
I care so little about this issue that I didn't call anybody, but just decided to talk to you callers.

Today is open-line Friday, when callers are under the illusion that they choose the topics.

There are no topics, sir. There are only issues and events that we discuss [on my radio show]. And you can make one up if you want.

I do not look at you people as customers.

Oh, no? From the Rush Limbaugh Merchandise catalog:

Signature Mug	**$16.00**
The "Legend" T-Shirt	**$18.00**
Golf Hat	**$15.00**
Golf Putter	**$90.00**
Bumper Sticker	**$2.00**
Rush "Relaxer" Mink Glove	**$90.00**
Window Stick Up	**$4.00**
Lapel Pin	**$4.00**
Wristwatch	**$40.00**
Magnet	**$5.00**
Diploma	**$35.00**
Sweatshirt	**$40.00**

You, too, can be an official Dittohead for only $359.00.

People who listen to this program are not mind-numbed robots.

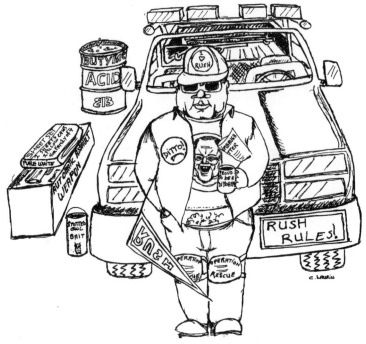

Here are a few in praise of the master:

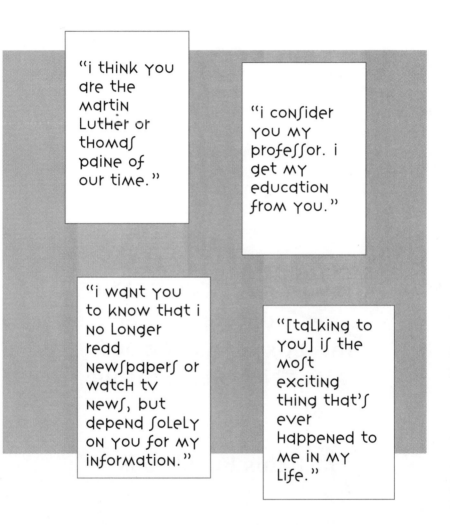

"i think you are the martin Luther or thomas paine of our time."

"i consider you my professor. i get my education from you."

"i want you to know that i no longer read newspapers or watch tv news, but depend solely on you for my information."

"[talking to you] is the most exciting thing that's ever happened to me in my life."

And then there was the comment from the landlord of a man who got arrested after trying to sell nearly $11,000 worth of explosives to undercover police: he "got all fired up" listening to Rush Limbaugh.

And then there are those among his "happy, carefree, and compassionate" followers, as Rush calls them, who send us at the *Flush Rush Quarterly* mail and messages such as these:

THE ONLY difference Between this box of manure and your "Newsletter" is the box!

Flush this Fuckheads

The first Rush room to be recorded on canvas. While the intellectual capacity of Dittoheads has deteriorated over the years, their spirit lives on. After *Comedians Dancing* by Pieter Quast, 1605-1647.

Brian,
You must be one real faggot. They and the rest of the freaks of the world are the only ones who oppose Rush. I would love to see you beaten bloody. Myself, when my friends and I go to Scum Francisco to beat up queers, we prefer to use the traditional thick broom handle. This is what I'll use on you if I get the opportunity.
Now, I don't agree 100% with Rush—he does lean to the left a bit too much. He's to [sic] nice. We've got to promote intolerance with passion—that will get this country back to where it belongs. We will return to the pre-1960 era in every way—mark my words.
Fuck you very much, [illegible signature]
P.S. May you die miserably—may it take a long time—you deserve to suffer.

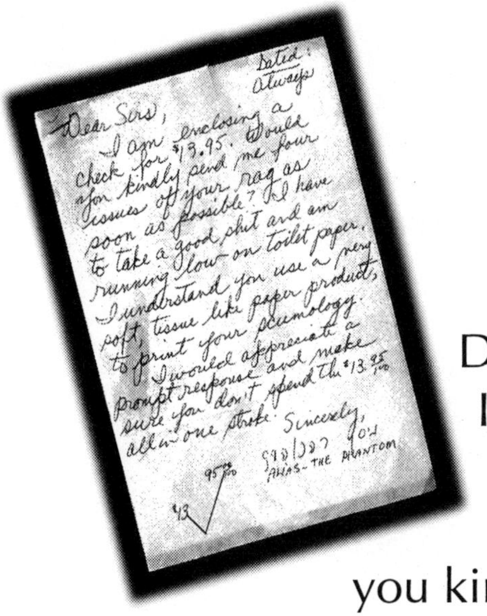

Dated: Always

Dear Sirs,
I am enclosing a check for $13.95. Would you kindly send me four issues of your rag as soon as possible? I have to take a good shit and am running low on toilet paper. I understand you use a very soft, tissue like paper product, to print your scumology.
I would appreciate a prompt response and make sure you don't spend the $13.95 all in one stroke.
Sincerely,
ALIAS - THE PHANTOM

Dear Sirs,
I am enclosing a check for $13.95. Would you kindly send me four issues of your rag as soon as possible? I have to take a good shit and am running low on toilet paper. I understand you use a very soft, tissue like paper product, to print your scumology.
I would appreciate a prompt response and make sure you don't spend the $13.95 all in one stroke.

Sincerely,
THE PHANTOM

Dear Bright Boy,

When I write a nasty letter, I usually give my name and address. This time I will not because I expect you are probably tied in with every lowlife in the country & have a variety of dirty tricks up your sleeve. That's what I expect from a fatheaded mick such as yourself. Some of the Irish (Buchanan, Buckley) overcome their nasty genes. The rest of you occupy your lives not with accomplishment, but with tearing down the accomplishments of others, drinking, fighting, union goon-ism and unrestrained self-pity. The latter is the hallmark of your people.

So I don't indent consistently. Big deal.

I want to suggest an editorial topic for your publication.

Is homosexuality: A) Wonderful?

B) Not wonderful, and therefore something that one should accuse others of (falsely) in order to get their goat?

I had better belabor this point, because I am dealing with idiots.

Homos say "Homosexuality is wonderful". Then, they go to great lengths to accuse people like Tom Selleck of being homosexual, falsely I might add. Why don't they make up their fucking minds? Is it a prideful or shameful thing? It seems to me, if you think homosexuality is good, then the way to get Tom Selleck's goat is to accuse him of being a heterosexual.

Other suggested topics:

1) How Clarence Thomas managed to sexually harrass Anita Hill 6 months before she started working for him.

2) The successes of Socialism. (filler item)

3) The pacifism of JFK, LBJ, Truman, FDR, Wilson and liberal Republicans (in name only) Lincoln and Teddy Roosevelt. (another filler item)

4) The benefits of raising the capital gains tax in the late 80's. (F.I.)

5) The benefits of the luxury tax. (F.I.)

6) Bill Clinton's idols in the world and history of economics.

7) The Greenhouse Effect as evidenced by 1993 temperatures in the USA. (F.I.)

8) The hypocrisy of the free-speech crowd as evidenced by the Political Correctness movement.

9) Marge Schott's freedom of speech.

10) The accomplishments of Rodney King. (maybe you need a little filler item)

11) Brian Kelliher: Asshole Fuckface Shiteating Self-Pitying Mick liberal Proponent of Big Government Gayboy

—Buttlips Van Regenmorter IV

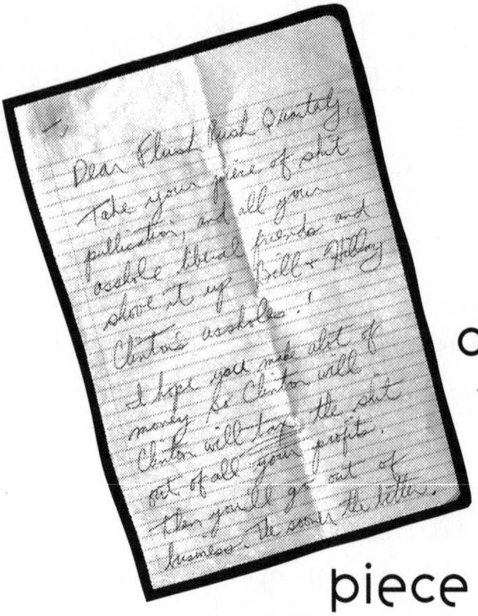

dear ꟻLUꟻH
ruꟻH
quarterLy,
take your
piece oꟻ ꟻHit
pubLicatioN, aNd aLL
your aꟻꟻHoLe LiberaL
ꟻrieNdꟻ aNd ꟻHove it up
biLL & HiLLary cLiNtoN'ꟻ
aꟻꟻHoLeꟻ.
i Hope you make aLot
[ꟻic] oꟻ moNey ꟻo
cLiNtoN wiLL cLiNtoN
wiLL [ꟻic] <u>tax</u> tHe ꟻHit
out oꟻ aLL your proꟻitꟻ.
tHeN you'LL go out oꟻ
buꟻiNeꟻꟻ. tHe ꟻooNer
tHe better.

66 I'm not leading the dog.
I'm on the tail end of it. **99**

SUBSCRIBE TO THE *FLUSH RUSH QUARTERLY*
If you enjoyed the book, you're going to love the newsletter.
Stay informed of the antics of the draft-dodging, mysogynistic, homophobic clown prince of the airwaves, who is a danger to our animal population and the environment and the American way of life.
Subscribe to the *Flush Rush Quarterly* by sending $13.95 for a one-year subscription to:
Flush Rush Quarterly
PO Box 270525
San Diego
CA 92198